YOU MUST!

You Must!

Basic Rules For Living The Best Life You Can

By

James Trotter

Trafford Publishing
Bloomington, IN

Order this book online at www.trafford.com
or email orders@trafford.com

Most Trafford titles are also available at major online book retailers.

Printed in Victoria, BC, Canada.

ISBN: 978-1-4269-2397-5 (sc)

Library of Congress Control Number: 2009913222

*Our mission is to efficiently provide the world's finest, most comprehensive
book publishing service, enabling every author to experience success.
To find out how to publish your book, your way, and have it available
worldwide, visit us online at www.trafford.com*

Trafford rev. 12/28/2009

Trafford PUBLISHING® www.trafford.com

North America & international
toll-free: 1 888 232 4444 (USA & Canada)
phone: 250 383 6864 ♦ fax: 812 355 4082

ACKNOWLEDGEMENTS

First I would like to thank my family. We are not perfect. However, in my opinion, we are 99.9% of the way there! My wonderful wife and our beautiful daughter mean more to me than anything else in this world. Thank you for your love and support, your patience, your attitudes, your smiles, and everything else about you. I love you both so much!

I would also like to thank Dr. Marcy Aycock. You are not just a great administrator; you are a great friend and a wonderful person. We are very fortunate to have you and your family in our lives. Thank you for teaching me when I come to you with unusual questions. Keep persevering and don't give up. The investment you have made in the lives of thousands of children will not be forgotten. We have leaned on you when we needed strength; please allow us to return the favor. We love you!

I can't forget about Sally Holliday. Thank you so much for the time and attention you have given our daughter. Your wisdom and counsel is something I prize very much. You give so much of yourself, and I want you to know that it is not unnoticed. Thank you for all that you have done for us, and for all the other children you have impacted so deeply. Thank you for your words of encouragement when I started writing this book, as well as while it progressed. You are also a great friend, and we hope to enjoy the friendship for a long time to come.

To Joe and Michelle Boyd. What can I say? I am so indebted to you both. Thank you for your friendship. Thank you for believing in us and letting us go with you and grow with you. You both are fantastic leaders, and your transparent hearts and spirits make people gravitate toward you. We are your biggest fans! We love you both so much and can't imagine our lives without you. I hope we have decades to share together here on earth, and I know we have all eternity in heaven once we leave these "tents" behind. Thank you for being you!

Lastly, I would like to thank Diana Fisher and Sarah Nienke. Your cowardly, dishonest, unethical behavior knocked me down, but not out. In fact, it had the opposite effect. It forced me to stand on my own two feet; to reach higher, push harder, dig deeper, and decide for myself what would become of my future. I stand tall today and say that I am proud of myself, and I know that others are proud of me as well. I hope that you do not put anyone else through what you put me through. However, it may just be the catalyst needed to push someone else to higher levels of success as it did for me.

INTRODUCTION
PLEASE READ THIS (!)

If you are like me, you are not necessarily fond of book introductions. I would much rather get on with the reading of the actual book! However, from time to time, I find myself being very thankful that I have taken the time to read what the author (or a person specifically chosen to write an introduction for a particular book) has to say. Perhaps he sheds some light on the history of the persons in the book. Or maybe it is the history of the location that helps clarify why certain things happen or are said. Sometimes, an introduction explains that certain characters in a work of nonfiction are in fact fictitious. This is due to several characters being combined into one (called a composite character) which saves having to write the same things over and over about multiple characters, which in turn saves time.

In the case of this book, it seems that a brief introduction is necessary to point out that the book seems to go in reverse order. In other words, the last chapter is what you should do first, and the first chapter is the last step. When you read the first paragraph of the first chapter, you may be tempted to put the book down and do something you have wanted to do for quite some time but had not yet gotten around to it. I would say that's great, but I would also caution against it.

The book is written in a particular order (which you will see and understand after reading the first few chapters) and builds upon itself with each subsequent chapter and topic. For this reason, you should read the book in its entirety and without skipping around. By reading every chapter and reading them in the order they are written, you will find that each step (chapter) compliments the preceding and builds to a natural culmination.

So why write a book in reverse order in the first place? Actually, there are a couple of reasons. The first chapter became the first chapter because of its importance. If you don't follow the advice in chapter one, the other chapters just don't mean as much. Chapters 2 – 6 just fell into place as logical steps, each building on the previous.

Likewise, the last chapter also is a natural first step and precursor to the preceding chapters, and, because of its importance, it should stand out in your mind. Thus, the first and last chapters have their preeminence in position in the book: The first chapter grabs your attention and is the most important step, and the last chapter (because it is the last chapter) sticks in your memory because you read it last, and because it is the first step.

You will also notice that this is an admittedly short book; only seven chapters. This ties in nicely with the fact that there are seven days in a week. If you should so choose, once you have read the book through, you can read one chapter a day for seven straight days. This is something I have found to be quite useful for me, and I have things that I read every day. It only takes a few minutes to read the things I read, and I typically read them when I wake up and before I go to sleep. I encourage you to come up with your own reading schedule and find what works best for you.

Again, because of the brevity of this particular book, you will find that reading one chapter a day will not typically take more than 5 or 10 minutes. Then you can read something else if you have it, or that can be all. The choice is yours. However, I would encourage you to read. In fact, one entire chapter of this book is devoted to reading and the importance of it.

Let me say once again that I am not a big fan of introductions, so this is the end of this one. Read the book, enjoy it, and build on it if you want to. I wish you all the best, and may God richly bless you!

TABLE OF CONTENTS

Let me just say these things are not bad. You need to be sincere. You need to have a desire, or in other words, you need to want to do something. If you want to do nothing, that's what you'll do. You need to know or feel that there's at least some chance of success. (This is not always the most important thing. Many of the things people have accomplished were done so when everyone else said it couldn't be done. Imagine telling someone in 1960 that a man would soon be walking on the moon. You might have literally been laughed out of the building, or even out of town! Yet, one decade later, men walked on the moon, not just once, but several times over! But that's another story. Just remember the old saying, "If you can dream it, you can do it!" But a little common sense and doing your homework also goes a long way. Someone once said, "There are two kinds of people in the world: doers and thinkers. The thinkers need to do more and the doers need to think more.")

Unfortunately, most of these people have one more thing in common: They did not take action. They were sincere. They truly believed change was coming, and they sincerely wanted that change to come! They had a desire to make a change, and reasons why the change would be good. And they had evidence that it could be done (in most cases), and in some cases, had even seen the evidence first hand by someone close to them making good on *their* resolutions. So what happened? The sincerity, the desire, and the evidence were just not enough. You've heard it before, and you will hear it again: You must take action!

All the sincerity your soul can muster, with all the desire of all the people in the world, put together with all the evidence anyone could ever need, is still useless without action! It's like starving at a Las Vegas buffet. The food is there, but you must eat! Without the action of putting the food in your mouth, you will die of starvation surrounded by mountains of food. "What irony!" some would say. "What foolishness!" others would say. "What a tragedy!" still others would say. They would all be right.

I like to read. One of the best books I have read is called "The Automatic Millionaire" by David Bach. The book is great, and has lots of good ideas, strategies, advice, and "Aha moments." However, the thing I like the most about this book is the end of each chapter. This is how David put it in the book's introduction:

*"As you'll see in the next few hours, because of its unbelievably simple approach, this is an unbelievably easy book to get through. What's more, each chapter ends with a short summary outline I call **Automatic Millionaire Action Steps,** which makes crystal clear exactly what you can do today to start yourself on the road to accumulating real wealth."*[1]

There are a few key words in the paragraph above. First, each chapter contains the Action Steps. Not some, or half, or most of the chapters; each one has a place where it says, "Take action!" Second, the action steps are what you can do today. Stop waiting. Stop worrying. Stop playing the "what if" game. General George Patton said, "A good plan violently executed today is far and away better than a perfect plan tomorrow." Your plan of action may not be perfect, but that's OK. Go! Do it! Today!

"But what if I fail?" Everyone faces failure. The question is, what will you do when you encounter it? Only you can determine whether the failure overcame you, or you overcame the failure. Grace Hopper said, "A ship in port is safe, but that's not what ships are built for." You will never accomplish what you want if you are only concerned about safety and security. Failure is not final or fatal unless you allow it

---

1 "The Automatic Millionaire" David Bach, Broadway Books

to be. Remember the words of Henry Ford: "Failure is the opportunity to begin again, more intelligently."

Third, the action steps are clear. They are not complicated, multi-step processes that involve lots of time and attention. In some cases the action is simply to decide. Right here, right now, decide. As the actor and brilliant economist Ben Stein said, "The indispensable first step to getting the things you want out of life is this: decide what you want."

So, are you going to take action, or are you going to continue to make excuses and tell yourself once again all the reasons you can't do it? Ben Stein also said, "So many fail because they don't get started – they don't go. They don't overcome inertia. They don't begin." Eugene F. Ware said, "All glory comes from daring to begin." Successful people don't make excuses; they make things happen.

You can't be lazy. Lazy people don't enjoy success. Success comes to those who work for it. It's been said that luck is the point where hard work and opportunity come together. Dr. Armand Hammer said, "When I work fourteen hours a day, 7 days a week, I get lucky." Please don't think that I am suggesting that everyone work fourteen hours a day, seven days a week. What I am suggesting is that it is the hard work that creates "luck". The author, speaker, and teacher Diana Rankin said, "It takes twenty years of hard work to become an overnight success." Another great quote by Ray Kroc: "Luck is a dividend of sweat. The more you sweat, the luckier you get." Let's not forget about Lucille Ball. She said, "Luck to me is something else. Hard work – and realizing what is opportunity and what isn't." And finally, a quote from one of our great founding fathers, Thomas Jefferson, who said, "I'm a great believer in luck, and I find the harder I work, the more I have of it." Obviously I'm not alone in thinking that work may be a key to "being lucky".

The title of this chapter is "Swoosh!" It is inspired by the Nike shoe company. That little symbol on their shoes, apparel, boxes, and everything else they produce is called the Nike Swoosh. Every time you see the Nike swoosh, you probably remember their motto; "Just Do It". You don't have to figure that out. You don't have to have that explained to you. You don't have to find the deeper meaning in it. I like that. It's simple. And so is this: Go! Get out there! You must take action!

GOAL!!!!!

CHAPTER 2
YOU MUST HAVE A GOAL

Have you ever watched or listened to soccer games from Latin American countries? First of all, the commentators seem to speak so fast! I'm sure it's just because I don't understand the language, but it really seems fast! (I often wonder if they think the same thing about Americans, but that's another story.)

Second, they are excited! When the ball is getting close to the goal, they start raising the pitch of their voices, the volume, and (somehow) the speed! But the best part is when someone gets the ball into that net. The commentator screams, "GOOOOOAAAAAALLLLLLL!!!!!!" It's fun to watch and listen to.

So what's the point? The point is, without the bars sticking up with the net wrapped around them (i.e. the goal), it really wouldn't be that exciting. I mean, let's face it. Without the goal, it would just be a bunch of people kicking a ball around a grassy field. *BORING!* It's the goal in any game that makes that game worth watching. And playing! Without the goal, it's useless.

I remember some years ago I was at a seminar. The speaker was one of my favorite people to listen to and I was enjoying his presentation. He asked for a volunteer from the audience and a friend of mine raised his hand when I raised mine. (We'll say my friend's name is Mike.) The speaker chose Mike to go up on stage and help illustrate a point. Mike jumped up on stage right in the middle in front of the audience (instead of taking the stairs on the side. He's such a show-off).

As soon as Mike was up there, the speaker ducks behind the curtain and pulls out a basketball. He hands it to Mike and says something like, "We're going to see if you are any good at basketball. So go ahead and shoot." Mike looks around for a second or two and then turns back to the speaker and asks the perfect question. "Where's the goal?" (I think that's why I didn't get chosen. I would have asked some stupid question like, "So, you got some string and wood so I can throw something together real quick?" It just wouldn't have been the same.)

"Where's the goal?" Mike asked. The speaker says, "Thank you very much." He dismisses Mike back to his seat, and we all learn a very valuable lesson. If you don't know what you're shooting at, how do you know if you make it? If you don't know where you're going, how do you know when you get there? If you don't know what the goal is, how do you know if you've achieved it?

I remember hearing a story about a gas station attendant who is putting gas in a car one afternoon. He looks up and sees a guy running straight toward him at full speed. Breathing heavily and sweating profusely, the runner stops for a quick breather near the attendant who has just finished filling the car. The attendant looks at the runner and asks, "Where you going?" To which the runner responds, "I don't know, but I'm getting there fast!" The attendant asks the obvious question, "How do you know?" The runner stands in stunned silence, realizing that if he doesn't know where he's going, how can he be sure he's not running in the wrong direction?!?!

You may have heard it before, but it is worth repeating. The top three percent of successful people have this in common: they have a goal, and it is written down and reviewed daily. Again, I like action. So if you don't have a goal written down so you can review it daily, do yourself a favor and go do that right now. A goal is so important, as illustrated in the examples above. However, if the goal is not written down, it isn't so much a goal as it is a dream. Please don't misunderstand. A dream is something you need, and I think you should have one (or more) and it should be big! However, the way to achieve your dreams is to set goals.

Think of goals as measurable steps toward reaching something bigger. Let me give you an illustration. Let's say your dream is to go to Hawaii. (If you live in Hawaii, let's say your dream is to go to New York.) One of your first goals may be to save $1,000 dollars this year, next year, and the following year. The next goal is to do the research on the best places to stay while you're on the islands. The next goal is to find out who you know that has gone before and get information from them on things like attractions, fun things to do and see, and so forth. The next goal would be to begin planning your schedule (putting in vacation time requests at work, for example). Each of these things is a measurable step toward something bigger, i.e., going to Hawaii. Hawaii is the dream; saving, planning, researching, and scheduling are goals: measurable steps to realize the dream. If you don't have any goals, you basically just have a "happy place" in your mind (and you probably won't ever make it to Hawaii).

Maybe you've heard the old saying, "How do you eat an elephant? One bite at a time." A goal is to take so many bites per day until the whole elephant has been eaten. By looking at the elephant as a whole, you become overwhelmed. You start thinking, "There's no way! It's just too big." By setting goals, you can focus on each step of the journey toward reaching the end. Goals help you adjust your focus from the large, overwhelming end picture, down to the steps that you can do each day (or week, or month, or whatever) until the final objective is reached. The famous director Cecil B. DeMille said, "The person who makes a success of living is the one who sees his goal steadily and aims for it unswervingly."

Again let me say that a goal is different from a dream. I think everyone should have dreams, and I think those dreams should be written down and reviewed also. But if you have dreams with no goals to achieve those dreams, why have the dreams in the first place? If you have dreams, great! Now determine if you have goals to meet those dreams. If not, stop right now and set some goals! Seriously, stop reading and set some goals right now. And then write them down and review them every single day.

Don't just kick the ball around a grassy field with your coworkers for your whole life. You must set goals and take action!

"The buck stops here."

CHAPTER 3
YOU MUST TAKE PERSONAL RESPONSIBILITY

P resident Harry Truman had a philosophy about passing the buck: He didn't. The importance of personal responsibility cannot be overstated. This is something I learned a little about some time ago.

Personal responsibility comes into play in every area of your life. Think about it for just a moment. Getting up on time, getting to work on time, getting the job done, getting the kids picked up, getting the errands done, getting the laundry done, getting the bills paid, getting enough sleep, not sleeping too much and wasting the day, not over eating, exercising regularly, going to the doctor and dentist and optometrist regularly. There is so much that depends on you being responsible. And yet, so many people pass through life as if everything is someone else's responsibility.

I have to admit, this is a big pet peeve of mine. Perhaps I should apologize now if this chapter seems a bit too harsh. I don't mean to be critical, and remember I'm not preaching at you, I'm learning with you. Personal responsibility is something I also have to remember and work on frequently.

Unfortunately, we live in a very litigious society. Everybody is a "victim". Around three-fourths of the world's lawyers practice here in the United States and somewhere around 95% of the worlds lawsuits are filed here as well. What a sad statistic! Why is it always someone else's fault? Because nobody wants to take personal responsibility any more. This is so aggravating and frustrating to me. I know it sounds weird, but I actually like it when people point it out to me if I seem to be trying to pass the buck and not take responsibility for something. Unlike most people, I want to improve. I want to be better. I want to be a person that people know they can count on. I'm not perfect, but I'm trying to improve all the time.

I remember some time ago I was talking with a friend of mine who was overweight. We'll say his name is Tom. Tom and I played racquetball together, we had a membership to the same gym, and we both had exercise equipment at home. The difference between us, however, was that Tom always seemed to do the minimum. He would play racquetball a couple times a week, but only for 30 to 45 minutes.

Now, for those of you who don't know much about racquetball, it is a pretty fast paced game and can get quite intense. The problem is, it requires very fast bursts of speed and energy and then some down time when the ball is dead and it becomes someone's serve. Consequently, the heart does not always stay in what is called "the target zone" for a long enough time to be an effective fat-burning exercise. You can burn up to 800 calories during one hour of racquetball, but if you're not playing that long or too intensely, obviously you will not see that kind of result.

Another good fat-burning exercise is just walking. Tom and I both have treadmills and would use them occasionally. Again, the goal is to get your heart rate in "the target zone" for at least 20 minutes so that the exercise begins to do some good. This means you should have somewhere around a 5 to 10 minute warm-up, then a minimum of 20 minutes with your heart rate in "the target zone", then another 5 to 10 minutes to cool down, depending on the level of your exercise. (It should be noted here that I am not a doctor or nutritionist or health expert in any way. What I am sharing here is what I have been told and still follow to this day. It may not be right for you, and I highly encourage you to speak to your doctor, or at least a personal trainer at your local gym [this is usually free if you have a membership] before starting or changing your personal fitness routine. Every body is different, and you should get expert advice for your body type and current fitness level.)

Aside from having your heart rate in "the target zone" for a minimum of 20 minutes each time you exercise, you should be doing this 4 to 6 days a week (again, this is what I have been told). Tom would walk on his treadmill the minimum of 20 minutes a day (no warm-up or cool-down), and he would only do this 2 or 3 days a week. Then he would complain to me that he wasn't seeing the results he really wanted. I remember telling him, "Tom, you can't do it half way. There are minimums you have to meet. If you aren't meeting them, you will never see the results you want."

Guess what happened? Tom actually got mad at me! He said he tried, but he really didn't enjoy walking on his treadmill. And the racquetball should be doing some good, shouldn't it? The truth is, yes! *IF* you are getting and keeping your heart rate in "the target zone" for the minimum amount of time, each and every time you play. As far as enjoying walking on the treadmill (or not), that's something you will have to figure out.

Not everything you do is enjoyable. Some things have to be done just because they have to be done. Does everyone enjoy getting up and going to work every day? Probably not! But people must go to work. Does everyone enjoy cleaning? Probably not! But you can't live in filth. Does everyone enjoy exercising? Probably not! But people must exercise to stay healthy.

Just because you don't enjoy doing it doesn't mean you can skip out on your responsibility to get it done!

I warned you I might get a little harsh.

Let me give you an example of my own personal responsibility learning curve.

I love crystal. Crystal vases, crystal collectibles, crystal chandeliers, whatever it is, if it's crystal, I like it! Our house is filled with crystal of all kinds. I have crystal candy dishes, and gravy boats, and candle holders, and ice buckets, and of course all of the normal crystal things like vases and stemware. I also have quite a few crystal pitchers and decanters. I like crystal so much I even started a company, The Beauty Of Crystal. You can visit the website at www.beautyofcrystal.com. There you will see a lot of the pieces that are currently "on display" in my living room, dining room, and kitchen.

One evening, we were having a party at our house and my wife was washing up a few things in the sink before people arrived. One of our friends showed up early and graciously offered to help us get things ready before the rest of the crowd got there. (We *love* to entertain, so a party at our house is almost always quite an affair.) One of the things that still needed to be done was to have a decanter rinsed out since it had been in the cabinet for a while. I got the decanter out and set it on the counter where my wife and friend were working near the sink.

I still don't know exactly what happened. All I heard was the crash. My friend screamed, my wife gasped, and I ran to see what was going on. Sure enough, my crystal decanter (one of my favorites, which is why I chose that particular one to use that night) was in pieces in the sink. My friend almost began to cry, knowing that I loved crystal and that this was a piece that meant a lot to me. She began to apologize profusely and swear that she would replace it as soon as she could. I told her it would be OK, and not to give it another thought.

(Fortunately for me, I had learned somewhere along the way that a friend is always more precious than any material possession. Sure I was upset about the decanter, but was it worth throwing away a dear friend for something so easily replaceable as a decanter from my local mall? Not a chance!)

I thought about it all night. "Why wasn't she more careful? What was she doing that caused the decanter to end up broken? Why didn't she move it if she was going to be doing something that would raise the chances of something happening to it? How could she have been so careless?" Then it hit me. "Who put the decanter right in front of her in the first place?"

I did.

I chose to put that decanter right in front of where she was working. I chose to take the chance of something happening to it. I am the one who must take personal responsibility for the decanter getting broken.

Why did I set it there? I saw them working there. If I had taken the time to think about it, I should have known that right in front of them may not be the best place to put a fragile, very breakable crystal decanter. Duh!

The next night, I apologized to her for putting that decanter in her way. But more than that, I apologized to her for making her feel so bad because she had broken the decanter when she actually had very little to do with it. I knew she felt horrible, and that made me feel horrible. It simply wasn't her fault. It never would have happened if I hadn't set it there. The responsibility was mine. Fortunately, I was able to see that. I have learned from that experience, and I will never forget it.

(P.S. – I found and bought another decanter that I like even better. It's *gorgeous*! You should see it. Maybe we'll have another party and invite some of my readers. And I'll keep the decanters away from the workers!)

I understand life isn't fair and sometimes things happen that are beyond your control. I have experienced that first hand on more than one occasion.

In December of 2002, I was "downsized" right out of a very good job with a large company. (I was also working a part-time job in the evenings when I got the news that our department was closing. My boss at my part-time job did me a huge favor and let me come on board full time.) Literally overnight, I took a 49% pay cut, lost all health insurance and benefits, and had to start all over in a new career.

In May of 2009, I was fired from another good job (which I really liked) because I answered a question wrong. Nothing illegal. Nothing unethical. I just answered a question wrong and six days later I was fired. I was informed that, because of what had happened, the company needed to make "organizational changes." (Apparently that is some kind of corporate code for "We really have no reason to fire you, but you're leaving anyway.")

Life is not fair. I know that. But are you going to sit around complaining about the unfairness of life, or are you going to take responsibility for your future, get back on your feet and move on? The choice is yours.

Your future is in your hands. Life may hand you all kinds of things, but it is what you do with them that makes the difference. Mike Murdock, another of my favorite speakers, once said, "You don't drown by falling in the water. You drown by staying there." You can be or do or have or achieve whatever you want. Just make up your mind to do it, and know that your future does not depend on someone else. If you get knocked down, get back up and get going again.

You must take personal responsibility, set some goals, and take action!

"The source is within!"

CHAPTER 4
YOU MUST REALIZE WHERE
MOTIVATION COMES FROM

I love quotes. You may know that if you have actually read all the pages before this one. People have the ability to inspire other people to do incredible things with just a spoken word. One of the reasons I love quotes is because I'm really not that smart. If I can use someone else's words and sound smart, great! One of my favorite quotes that I say to myself (a lot!) is, "A wise man knows that he is not that wise." The one thing I can say about myself is this: I'm just wise enough to know that I am not that wise.

While I love quotes, I have learned that quotes and sayings and things like that have the ability to become a sort of crutch. As long as you have access to quotes, you can stay inspired. But when the quotes are out of sight, they are also typically out of mind. If they are not in mind, you don't stay inspired, and you revert back to your old attitudes and behaviors. What happens then? You're right back where you started. If you're reading the quotes, you're feeling good. If you're not reading the quotes, you're not so good.

Maybe I'm different than most other people. Maybe most people can read a few quotes and then they're good for the rest of their life. I find that a little hard to believe, but I'm trying to give the benefit of the doubt. To me it seems kind of like going to a gym and working out once and thinking, "I'm fit for life!" Most likely, no.

I have learned that for me, motivation comes from within. I love to read quotes because they remind me that other people in the world have been through tough times and have risen above. Most people in the world have gone through tougher times than I have. When I remember that, it's easy to get back on track and stop feeling like the world is picking on me. Quotes can quickly and easily snap me back into reality.

That being said, I should also say that inspiration is great, depending on what you do with it. If you are watching TV and reading quotes during the commercials and then going right back to watching TV, it seems pretty obvious that the quotes are doing little for you and will continue to do little for you until you make some changes. Like I said earlier; if you want to do nothing, that's what you'll do.

If, on the other hand, you use that inspiration to fuel the motivation that you have inside of you, your motivation can increase and you can begin to do things that most people would never even attempt. Great things have been done in this world because someone was inspired, and then paired that inspiration with their own motivation, took action, and made a change.

In chapter 1, I said that desire alone is not enough. Some might disagree with that statement, but please hear me out.

If your desire is strong enough to increase your motivation, and the motivation causes you to take action, then desire alone may be considered to be enough. However, if your desire is strong enough to increase your motivation, but not strong enough to increase your motivation enough to take action, then it can also be said that desire is not enough. It's a bit of a puzzle. What you need to understand is that desire paired with motivation that causes action is the bottom line.

Desire = A want for something.

Motivation = The incentive for putting together a plan or design to accomplish that something.

Action = Actually doing or progressing toward something in a real and tangible way.

Without any one of these ingredients it just isn't the same. If you have no desire, what will you do? You may have an angry boss as your motivation, and you may take action to keep your job, but without desire you most likely will not have that burning inside of you to see it through completely and/or to the best of your ability.

Without motivation, your desire may be strong and you may be taking action. But without a plan to do it well and do it right, it might take much longer than necessary, or it may not get finished at all. You will simply quit because your motivation (incentive) is not there. The desire may still be there, in other words you still want what you want, but you have no more motivation so the task remains unfinished.

Without action, well, we've already covered that. Suffice to say, without action, it's all just talk. Are you talking or are you doing?

Let's go back to Tom for just a moment. I told you earlier that Tom got mad at me for telling him he was going to have to kick it up a notch or two and stop doing it halfway. Actually, he was downright angry. Tom blamed me for his attitude and work ethic when it came to working out. He said something like, "Well I would walk more, but I don't see you picking up the phone and calling me to meet you at the gym!"

I was speechless. Tom clearly didn't understand that motivation comes from within. If he is always going to be waiting on someone else to get him to do what he should be doing on his own, he's not ever going to achieve much. By recognizing the fact that "the source is within" Tom wouldn't need me (or anyone!) to be calling him so that he does what he's supposed to do.

I hope you are not like that. And if you are, please begin to change. Again, you are in charge of you. If you have a desire to do something (if you have a want), then look inside and see what will motivate you to work toward that (determine your incentive), and then take action (work toward it in some tangible way). Remember, you can be or do or have or achieve whatever you want!

I believe that quotes and motivating and inspiring sayings can be a powerful tool. As I stated earlier, they can help me do a quick attitude adjustment, get me thinking right again and help me to keep moving forward. Just don't let them become a crutch; something you always have to have in order to keep going.

Motivation is internal, and very personal. You must realize where motivation comes from, then take responsibility, set some goals, and take action!

"Those who listen to instruction will prosper."
Proverbs 16:20

CHAPTER 5
YOU MUST BE TEACHABLE

Being teachable is so important! No matter what area of your life you want to improve or make changes to, you will most likely fail if you are not teachable. In fact, it should probably be restated to say that you <u>will</u> fail if you are not teachable. If you are going to do something different, in whatever area of your life, how will you expect to achieve any level of success at your new endeavor if you are not willing to learn something new about it? It simply will not work.

Being teachable literally means you are capable of being taught something. You are apt and willing to learn. Stop for a moment and ask yourself, "Am I really ready to learn? Am I willing to learn? Am I able to learn?" If the answer is no, you've got a tough road ahead.

"Am I ready to learn?" Has life beaten you up enough yet? Are you ready to try a new approach? Are you ready to stop doing the same thing and expecting different results? Are you ready to get out of that vicious circle? "I work hard so I can make more money, so I can have nicer things. Which means I have to work more, which means I have more money, which means I can have nicer things. Which means I have to work more, which means I have more money, which means I can have nicer things. Which means I have to…" UGH!! Home to work, work to home. Home to work, work to home. Are you exhausted? Are you in a rut? Is it a deep rut? What's the difference between a rut and a grave?

"Am I willing to learn?" Are you willing to try something new, even if you don't know what you're doing? Are you willing to listen to someone you may not know very well? Are you willing to learn from your mistakes, and more importantly, from the mistakes of others? Remember the old saying, "Learn from other people's mistakes. Life's too short to make them all yourself!" Are you willing to take instruction and maybe some criticism from someone else who has more experience, knowledge, and wisdom? (I'm not talking about being someone's doormat. I'm talking about taking constructive criticism without getting bent out of shape.) Are you willing to admit you don't have all the answers, especially in a new field of endeavor? These are tough questions that deserve an honest answer.

"Am I able to learn?" Are you so set in your ways that you just can't learn something new? Are you a know-it-all who already has all the answers, you just don't use them for whatever reason? If you are getting advice, do you shut down because you "don't want to listen to this guy! Who does he think he is?! He's just wrong!" Remember it is not just being ready and willing to learn. If you are not able to learn, in other words if your attitude just won't allow it, then you will stay in the same circumstances and situation that you are in right now until you become teachable.

This is what psychologist Dr. Scott Baker said, which he learned from many years of teaching martial arts:

"The student's attitude is the most significant aspect of their nature which contributes to either their success or failure in learning this complex system of skills. Attitude has a greater impact upon a student's success than natural ability and physical capacity. One can build capacity and endurance, and one can teach skills and abilities even to the untalented, but one cannot teach the un-teachable!

All your natural talent, your eagerness and hard work, your willingness to pay the price to master a skill, all of this amounts to little or nothing if you do not have an attitude that enables you to be taught. Most of the great instructors I have seen deal with the un-teachable student in much the same way. They leave them alone; let them spout off their great knowledge, and often do not correct what is wrong or confirm what is right. Remember this, if you are talking, then you are not learning, that is, with one exception: If you are asking questions, then you are in a learning dialogue with your teacher. Most competent teachers encourage students to ask questions."

Being teachable means you are open to taking counsel, and putting those words of wisdom into practice. This could be advice, instruction, criticism, or even opinions. Remember that everyone sees things from their own viewpoint. Ray Silverstein, founder and president of the Presidents Resource Organization, said, "What is obvious to one person may not be obvious to someone who doesn't have the same experience or perspective. All of us together are smarter than any one of us." It is hard to measure exactly how much you can benefit from the ability to gain insight and wisdom from those whose perspective and experience is different from yours. In fact, it may well be said that it is immeasurable.

One of the people that I like to listen to and glean wisdom from is Kevin Trudeau. He talks a lot about what he calls the "teachability index". It's very simple, and I encourage you to learn more about it. There are two parts to the index and, by rating yourself, you can determine just how teachable you are.

The good news is, even if you find you are not high (or even if you are very, very low) on the teachability index, you can change! Being teachable means opening up and exploring new options. It means asking questions. It doesn't mean you are going to change everything about yourself overnight. However, if you can just start asking questions, you are on your way to becoming teachable and getting more out of life. Like I said earlier, you are in charge of you. My friend Bob Woods used to tell me, "If you want to make some changes in your life, you need to make some changes in your life."

Being teachable is only half of the equation. You must also continue to learn. What good would it do to be teachable but never learn something new? In other words, if you're not going to continue to learn, why be teachable?

John Fallon is a teacher at Walhalla High School in Walhalla, South Carolina. He is also a public speaker and a consultant. You can see some of his slide shows at www.slideshare.net/fallonj, or you can visit his website at www.johnfallonpresents.com. He has a slide in one of his presentations that is very helpful. It is called:

5 Tips For Lifelong Learning[2]

1. *Find and work with a mentor.*

2. *Accept constructive criticism.*

3. *Engage in continuing education.*

4. *Get involved with a group of like-minded people.*

5. *Ask questions.*

1. **Find and work with a mentor.** A mentor is someone who imparts wisdom that they have learned themselves, either from their mentor or from their own past experiences. A mentor is a guide, a counselor, a teacher. A mentor usually wants you to be successful because it means they will be successful as well. (Not to mention the harm that may be done to their reputation if they mislead you.) Your best interests are usually their best interests. They can guide you around pitfalls and dangers that you don't know exist. I would strongly encourage you to diligently find and work with a mentor.

Also, do your homework when looking for a mentor. Interview them. Have they mentored anyone before? Do they have a mentor themselves? Can they tell you about past successes? Again, be diligent. Don't take the first person who comes along and says, "Sure, I'll be your mentor!"

A good book that I will recommend to you is *"As Iron Sharpens Iron"* by Howard and William Hendricks. This will help get you going in the right direction when it comes to finding the right mentor.

2. **Accept constructive criticism.** Again, this does not mean being someone's doormat. It does mean listening when someone who cares about you and your future tells you something

---

2 Used with permission from John Fallon. John's original list has been modified for use here.

you don't necessarily want to hear. It is very hard to do (trust me, I know!), but you will be better for it. Especially if it comes from your mentor who only wants you to be as successful as you can be. Try putting yourself in their shoes; to see why they are telling you what they are telling you. Remember, perspective makes a world of difference!

3. *Engage in continuing education.* This can be anything from books, to college credit hours, to meetings and seminars, tapes or CD's, anything! You should always want to continue to get better. There's a great line in the movie, "The Shawshank Redemption". Morgan Freeman's character says, "Get busy living, or get busy dying." If you're not moving forward, learning, growing, progressing, you're dying. Ray Kroc, the founder of McDonalds as we know it, said, "As long as you're green, you're growing. As soon as you're ripe, you start to rot." And we all know that rotting things stink!

4. *Get involved with a group of like-minded people.* People who share your interests and ideas. People who share your passion. People who want some of the same things out of life that you want. This would be a great place to find a mentor! If you are in a room with like-minded people, chances are you will find someone who has been doing it for a while and can teach you something about what you want to learn. A great quote that backs up point number 3 above and this point is from Charles Jones, better known as Charlie Tremendous Jones. He said, "You are the same today that you are going to be five years from now except for two things: the people with whom you associate and the books you read."

5. *Ask questions.* We talked a little about this earlier but it bears repeating. Don't be afraid to ask questions. What's the worst that could happen? Someone might think you don't know what you're talking about? Guess what? You don't! That's why you're asking questions. Again, this is where a

good mentor makes all the difference. He knows you don't know everything. That's why he's there! Get a mentor who loves to be asked questions. Someone who loves to teach and help and inspire another person. Someone who doesn't tell you what to do, but shows you what to do by doing it first. Or, by doing it together with you.

By following these five simple steps, you can be well on your way to more success in life. You can enjoy more because you are learning more. You are learning about more. You are seeing more things in this world than you saw before. You are growing and changing and developing. Your world is getting bigger, better, and brighter.

You must be teachable and continue to learn, realize where motivation comes from, take responsibility, set some goals, and take action!

"Reading is to the mind what exercise is to the body."
Richard Steele

CHAPTER 6
YOU MUST READ BOOKS

Y ou must read books. Books change the way you see your world, your neighbors, your country, your family, yourself. Books affect your very soul. They change you from the inside out, even when you don't notice you are being changed. If you want to be successful, you want to read books.

Books have the ability to raise us up. They inspire us. They let us know what can be accomplished. They push us forward. Books transport us through time, space, and matter. Whatever book you are reading, that's where you are while you're reading that book. From the ancient lands Moses wrote about 6,000 plus years ago, to the futuristic planets and star systems other writers have seen only in their minds. Reading a book takes you wherever you want to go.

Reading changes your life forever. Reading gives you access to ideas and information, as well as characters and stories, both fictional and nonfictional. Reading broadens your world beyond your circle of influence (i.e., your workplace, your family, your community). You're exposed to the thoughts, feelings, and imaginations of writers from other times, places, cultures, denominations, ethnicities, creeds, beliefs, etcetera, etcetera.

The French philosopher and mathematician Rene` Descartes said, "The reading of good books is like a conversation with the best men of past centuries – in fact, like a prepared conversation, in which they reveal only the best of their thoughts." Books give you the thoughts and minds of other people without having to spend every second of every day with other people. They give you the best thoughts from those people whose words have been handed down, in some cases, from generation to generation. Wisdom, insight, humor, sadness, instruction, anything you can think of, is waiting for you somewhere in a book.

I should warn you that just to read any book is not the same as reading the right book. If you want to build a garage in your back yard, you probably should not read a fictional book like "Huckleberry Finn". Huck Finn is a great book, I've read it myself. However, will it get you closer to having a garage in your back yard? Most likely, no. You should probably read a book with a title like, "How To Build A Garage". That would be a good book for you for what you want to accomplish. If you want to become a teacher, "How To Build A Garage" may not be a good book for you (unless maybe you're going to be a shop teacher).

So how does a person know what they should be reading? First, I think there are some books that all people should read regardless of what they want in life. I will list some of them for you later, but just know that some books are good for all people. Not all books are good for all people (and how would you read them all anyway?!?), but I believe some books should be read by everyone.

Second, you should be looking for and reading books that pertain to your areas of interest. What is it that you want (or need) to learn more about? Building a garage? Investing? Becoming an entrepreneur? There are books on every subject imaginable. You just need to find which books are right for you right now. Then devote some time every day to reading.

OK, let's find out which books you should be reading. Again, there are some books that I think everyone should read. This is by no means an exhaustive list, and there are books out there that you may have read already that you think should be on this list that are not here. That's OK. If you want to add them and compile your own list, I encourage you to do so. There may also be books on this list which you have read and you don't think they should be on the list. That is also OK. Again, as long as you are reading and growing, that's the point.

The books you should be reading are:

1. *The Holy Bible*. Everyone should be reading and re-reading the Bible. The Bible is the only book that has every success principle within its pages. If you want to be successful, start here. Obviously I'm not saying you have to read the whole Bible before you start other books, or before you start taking action. What you should do is read a minimum of 4 chapters a day. If you read 3 chapters in the Old Testament and 1 chapter in the New Testament each day, you will be through the whole Bible in less than a year. (Reading 4 chapters in your Bible each day would be a great goal! Go write it down!)

I know some of you may be thinking, "Come on. Are you serious? I don't want to read the Bible!" That's fine. You don't have to. This is not a mandatory reading list, I'm simply suggesting the books that will teach the most and do the most good. If you don't read your Bible, that's OK. You'll miss out on incredible teaching and blessings you probably can't even imagine, but if that's what you want to do, the choice is yours.

2. *How To Win Friends And Influence People* by Dale Carnegie. In my opinion, this is one of the best books ever written for success. Don't just read it; ingest it. Read it, memorize it, and most importantly, live it. This book has practical advice for anyone and everyone, regardless of age, ambition, level of success achieved or desired, or anything else. Once you have read it, read it again. You should be reading your Bible daily and this book at least once a year, every year.

3. *The Automatic Millionaire* by David Bach. I wish this *was* required reading, and I wish every child in America and around the world would read it and put it into practice. To put it succinctly; the earlier you start, the better. Buy more than one copy: one for you and one for your child(ren). And then do what it says! If every working person followed David's advice, we would be in such great shape as a nation. Why aren't people listening to good advice and wisdom like what's in this book? I'm not sure, but don't be unwise and follow their lead. Simple strategy, easy to do, and a bright future for those with the discipline to start and stay with it. This is a great book!

4. *The Magic of Thinking Big* by David J. Schwartz. Another great book which teaches on a host of subjects that all come together for the purpose of teaching people how to be more successful in whatever endeavor

they choose. It also has "case studies" so to speak. Specific examples of people and what they did. Again, it's all about learning from other peoples' mistakes.

5. *Think And Grow Rich* by Napoleon Hill. Notice that the title is not "Work and Grow Rich." Work is a necessary ingredient to success in anything, but you must first think. You have to know what it is that you want to work at. You must first think about what you want, and then work toward getting it. Remember, it starts in your head.

6. *Success Through A Positive Mental Attitude* by W. Clement Stone and Napoleon Hill. Another good book which teaches that you must have your mind right before the rest will come together. You can't have a positive life with a negative mind!

7. *I Can. You Can Too!* and *Get It Together*, both by Mamie McCullough. I love reading Mamie's books. You can feel her energy and cheerful attitude right through the pages. These two books were some of the first books I read years ago when someone suggested I start reading books to be even more successful. It's a good thing these were among the first because they energized me and got me excited to read even more. Mamie's books are fun, practical, easy to read, and very encouraging. I hope you enjoy them as much as I did!

8. *The Go-Getter* by Peter B. Kyne. This short little book teaches you one thing, as evidenced by its subtitle: "A Story That Tells You How To Be One." It is only around 50 pages long, but don't let that fool you! It is a modern parable that is very powerful if you grasp the teaching within its pages and then put it into action.

9. *The Millionaire Next Door* by Thomas J. Stanley and William D. Danko. This is a great book that teaches

some very surprising things about millionaires and what they do and don't do. It teaches about high consumption and low consumption lifestyles. You will learn whether you are a PAW, a UAW, or an AAW. (You'll understand these once you read the book.)

10. ***Rich Dad, Poor Dad*** and ***Increase Your Financial IQ***, both by Robert Kiyosaki. These are great books to help you become more financially literate. Good teaching, good advice, and good lessons in these books. Read them and then re-read them. You can never be too smart when it comes to money.

Again, this is not an exhaustive list. There are many other good books which I have read and recommend reading, such as "The Seven Habits of Highly Effective People" by Stephen R. Covey (excellent book I highly recommend), "It Only Takes Everything You've Got" by Julio Melara, "The Science of Success" by James A. Ray, "The 21 Success Secrets of Self-Made Millionaires" by Brian Tracy, "Principles and Success Strategies For Everyday Living" by Ralph Palmen, and "The Power of Positive Thinking" by Norman Vincent Peale. I have read these books and re-read them when I can. However, the books specifically listed above will get you jump-started on the path to success and wealth in a very short amount of time.

Read, re-read, and continue to read new books and information on your subject of choice. Leaders are readers. Not all readers are leaders, but all leaders are readers. Some readers are readers just for the joy of reading. However, if you see a person in a position of leadership or influence, I would bet they are an accomplished reader.

You must read books, be teachable and continue to learn, realize where motivation comes from, take responsibility, set some goals, and take action!

"The hardest arithmetic to master is that which enables us to count our blessings." Eric Hoffer

---

CHAPTER 7
YOU MUST COUNT YOUR BLESSINGS

Why do we spend so much time chasing more? Why is contentment so hard to find? Why do we so often forget about all the blessings we have been given? Most people would say it is because they have not been given many blessings. They could not be more wrong.

My daughter had an idea for an exercise. She said we should write down all the things that we were thankful for. My wife, our daughter and I all sat at the kitchen table and wrote down what we were thankful for. Before we started, I clarified that we should narrow it to some particular area of our lives that we were thankful for. I chose just my body, and my wife chose hers. Our daughter just started writing.

In just choosing this one thing, I filled an entire page of things that I could be thankful for. Stop for just a moment and think about it. Are you reading this book? That means you have sight (or tactile senses if you are reading this in Braille). You have mental capacity to know the words you are reading. You are probably holding the book in your hands, which means you have strength, at least to some degree. You have comprehension skills to give meaning to the thoughts you are taking in. In just the simple act of reading, you have at least these four blessings. There may be more that I have forgotten to list. Can you think of any other blessing that was not mentioned here? Perhaps the blessing of corrective lenses. How much more difficult would reading be if you didn't have glasses or contacts? Millions of people don't have that blessing. Are you counting it as one of yours?

Perhaps you don't have the ability to read this book yourself and someone is reading it to you. Aside from some of the blessings listed above, you have the blessing of a friend!

What if this is being read to you by some sort of electronic means, such as a computer? You still have the blessing of hearing along with the blessings listed earlier, and, *you have a computer!* What a blessing that is! Do you know what kind of wealth it takes to own a computer? Truly you are blessed!

"But wait" you say. "This isn't *my* computer. I'm just using the computer at my local library. I don't actually *own* a computer." So you have access to a computer, most likely free of charge, you know how to use that computer, and you are using it to better yourself. If you break it down and really look at it, this list of blessings will quickly go off the charts!

Do you see how blessed you are yet? Take about 10 to 15 minutes and just make a quick list of what blessings you think you have. I'll even let you cheat and give you some of my list! Here are some of the things I listed on my very first sheet within just a few minutes. And remember, this is just a list of things regarding me personally. If some of them don't apply to you, think of others. I'm sure I didn't get everything!

1. Eyesight

2. Hearing

3. Smelling

4. Tasting

5. Tactile senses (feeling things when you touch them)

6. Hair

7. Good health

8. Strength

9. The ability to breathe

10. Clean air to breathe

11. Sleep

12. Intelligence

13. Wisdom

14. Healthy skin

15. Healthy teeth

16. Healthy bones

17. Healthy joints

18. Healthy organs

19. Healthy circulatory system

20. Healthy immune system

21. Healthy digestive system

22. Healthy neurological and nervous system

23. Abilities in general (run, walk, jump, skip, lay down, sit up, etc.)

24. Emotions

25. Understanding / Comprehension

This is just a short list that, again, I came up with in less than a couple of minutes as I sit here writing this book! There are others that affect my body personally that are great blessings as well. Things like colors (what a wonderful blessing!), smells (some good, some not so much), food (tasting and enjoying it is one blessing, converting it to energy is many more, using it to build strength is yet another), sounds (beautiful music & poems, and warning sounds to keep you safe like train whistles and dogs barking), and different textures (rocks feel quite different than soft fleece or a down comforter and you know the difference between them just by putting your hand on them). Feeling is also in the skin in general, such as the difference in weather. Your body knows if you need a parka or a tank top. What a blessing!

If you are not thankful for the abundance of blessings you have been given already, why should you be entrusted with even more? If you are blind to the multitude of blessings you enjoy on a daily basis, most likely you will not be thankful when additional blessings come your way. I don't know about you, but if I consistently give things to a friend who is never appreciative, it won't be long before that friend gets nothing else from me!

Perhaps you have heard this saying before: Attitude is everything! Guess what? That saying is absolutely true. You need to be able to see how blessed you are, and then give thanks for being so blessed. And if you think you aren't blessed then go back and read the list you wrote (or at least go back and read the list I wrote for you and figure out how many of those apply to you).

If you are having trouble seeing how blessed you are, get out of your comfort zone and go visit a hospital. Go visit a special hospital such as a veteran's hospital or a cancer treatment hospital. Go serve for a couple of hours at a homeless shelter or "soup kitchen". Go drive through the poorer areas of your town and look at the houses that people live in because they can't afford to get something better. Read your newspaper or watch the news about what's going on around the world: famine, disease, war, terrorism. Do you see how blessed you are now?

Consider this: If you live in the United States of America, you're wealthy. Even the poor of this country are still better off than so many other people around the world. Just being here gives you blessings and opportunities that others don't have. If you don't think this is true, ask yourself why so many people are coming here (legally and illegally), leaving everything they have and risking their lives just to get to America. They understand that this is the land of opportunity and promise.

I'm not suggesting that America is perfect. America has her faults and failures, and sometimes our leaders let us down and go directions we shouldn't be going. However, as a whole, the USA is a beacon around the world. God has blessed us because we chose to honor Him. And those that continue to honor Him continue to see His blessings.

Here are just a few statistics to really point out how blessed you are:

- If you own a Bible, you are immensely blessed. About **one third** of the world does not even have access to a Bible, let alone own one.

41

- If you can attend a church meeting without the fear of harassment, arrest, torture, or death, you are more blessed than **three billion** people in the world.

- If you have never experienced the danger of battle, the loneliness of imprisonment, the agony of torture, or the pangs of starvation, you are ahead of **five hundred million** people in the world.

- If you woke up this morning with more health than illness, you are more blessed than the **one million people** who will not survive this week.

- If you have food in the refrigerator, clothes on your back, a roof over your head, and a place to sleep, you are richer than **75%** of the people in this world.

- If you have money in the bank, in your wallet or purse, and spare change in a dish, jar, or cup at home, you are among the top **8%** of the world's wealthy!

- If your household earns more than $45,000 annually, you are in the top **1%** of all wage earning households in the world. **The top one percent!**

The point is, blessings and opportunities abound, especially here in America. Just look at all you can do. Look at everything around you. Look in the mirror and see all the blessings you already possess. Now use those blessings and opportunities that you already have to create the future that you want. Fortunes are made by people who use their mental and physical abilities, their time, and their energy to create, rather than using it to complain. You have to ask and answer yourself honestly, "Which am I doing?" If you're complaining, chances are you're not counting your blessings.

Hannah More was an English religious writer and philanthropist who lived from 1745 to 1833. She wrote plays, became a teacher, and was active as a social reformer. One of the little poems she wrote is something I keep, and it reminds me that I am blessed even when I don't feel like it. It goes:

When thou has truly thanked the Lord

For every blessing sent,

But little time will then remain

For murmur or lament.

Hannah understood that when you take the time to really count all of your blessings, you won't have much time for grumbling and complaining. And to think she lived hundreds of years ago! No cell phones, (no phones at all!!), no TV, no internet, no modern appliances, modern medicine, technology, none of it! Yet, she knew how blessed she was and she shared whatever blessings she had with others. She set an example we should all be following.

OK, by now you should know that you are blessed. Whether you want to admit it or not, you are and there is nothing you can say or do to convince me otherwise. Now it's up to you. You have everything you need to be everything you want. In chapter one I said you must take action, and sometimes that action is just to decide. So, what are you going to do?

I will say it one last time: You are responsible for you. You can be or do or have or achieve whatever you want. You just have to determine what you want. Then, know that it is attainable. Abraham Lincoln said, "First let us determine that the thing can and will be done. Then we shall find the way." Whatever the "thing" is that you want, determine that you can and will succeed. Then it's just a matter of finding the right avenue to that leads you to it.

Well, this is it. I hope you find this information useful to you. I hope it has encouraged you to reach new levels of fulfillment. I wish you well in your endeavors, whatever they may be. As the English poet Francis Quarles said, "I wish thee as much pleasure in the reading as I had in the writing."

If you will allow, may I give you one last piece of advice? It is simply this:

You must count your blessings, read books, be teachable and continue to learn, realize where motivation comes from, take responsibility, set some goals, and take action!

Good luck and may God bless you!

EPILOGUE

Let me take just a moment to say thank you for taking some time to read this book. It is my sincere hope that you have learned something and will apply that learning to make a difference in your life. I do truly wish you all the success you want.

I should also point out that there are other things you should be doing to help with the journey on your way to living the best life you can. As I mentioned earlier, this book is not an exhaustive list, rather it is a starting point to get you thinking about what you can and/or should do. Consider this the building of, and launching pad for, the vehicle that will move you forward to whatever it is you want to be, do, have, or achieve. As the title suggests, these are basic things that everyone should do. However, there are other things that will also help you on your way, and I would encourage you to give these things some consideration as well.

First, you should get control of your finances. Money (or the lack thereof) is the number one reason for divorce in America. If you are not saving, start right now. Don't wait any longer. Learn how to live below your means. *Start* putting some money away and *stop* living paycheck to paycheck. It might be very difficult at first, but once you learn to do it you'll kick yourself for not doing it sooner.

Second, you should try to invest at least some small part of your income. It doesn't have to be a lot, and whatever you invest in does not have to be something super risky.

Speaking with a professional broker is always a good idea. They can show you all kinds of things, from strategies, to specific kinds of stocks, bonds, funds, and whatever else. Sometimes, the initial meeting is free. You have nothing to lose by looking into investing.

Next, you should know what you want to do and focus on it. If you are going in 10 different directions, you will be exhausted but not necessarily successful at any of the 10 things you're trying to get going. Pick something you want to do and then put everything you have into that. You will save yourself a lot of frustration, time, and anxiety. Focus is extremely important when starting something new. If you don't know what you want to do, then maybe you can do 10 things until you do figure out what you want to do. Then go with that and leave the other stuff alone until you are really going strong with the one thing you started earnestly focusing on.

One of the last things you should try to do is this: Be nice. In other words, be likeable. Try to be a person that other people like to be around and talk or work with. Don't gossip and don't be negative. Remember what your mother told you: If you can't say something nice, don't say anything at all. That reminds me of another of my favorite quotes. "Better to keep silent and be thought a fool than to open your mouth and remove all doubt." I'm sure you've heard the old saying, "Silence is golden." That saying holds true more than ever when it comes to rumors and gossip.

Another aspect of being a person that other people want to be around is good personal hygiene. Bathe every day. Brush your teeth every day. Dress for success. Use deodorant and perfume/cologne (in moderation, of course). No one wants to be around a funky-mouthed, dragon-breath'd person who doesn't bathe and dresses in inappropriate clothing. Take care of yourself. You're the only "you" you've got!

Again, I wish you all the success you desire. By following just a few basic rules, you will begin to see doors open and things happen that didn't seem possible before. Then it's up to you to walk through those doors and see what your future holds. Be excited! It only gets better! You just need to prove it to yourself!

www.ingramcontent.com/pod-product-compliance
Lightning Source LLC
Chambersburg PA
CBHW031008090426
42737CB00008B/727